T0115073

How to Overcome Your
FEAR OF CREATING

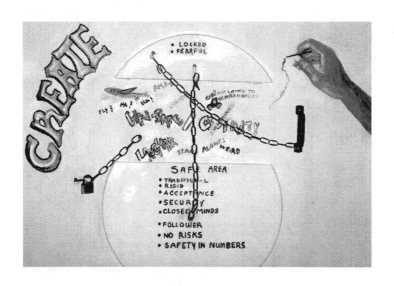

Barbara Gene

Order this book online at www.trafford.com
or email orders@trafford.com

Most Trafford titles are also available at major online book retailers.

Printed in the United States of America.

ISBN: 978-1-4669-7091-5 (sc)
ISBN: 978-1-4669-7092-2 (e)

Library of Congress Control Number: 2012922775

Trafford rev. 01/21/2013

 www.trafford.com

North America & international
toll-free: 1 888 232 4444 (USA & Canada)
phone: 250 383 6864 ♦ fax: 812 355 4082

For my mother, Risa Holloway, and my children: Theresa, Donald, Tammi, and Kenneth.

To all my ancestors, who fought for our freedom to read and write which made me strong and determined to communicate not only through writing, but also painting.

CONTENTS

ILLUSTRATIONS

FIGURES

FOREWORD

In this time of competition, everyone is striving to develop their own creativity. This book will hopefully inspire you to see your projects in a different light. You will be able to think of ideas, not only in the realm and perspective of the art world, but also through the eyes of an entrepreneur.

I took classes in criminal justice and saw the causes and results of fear and how it affected creativity.

After growing up, I now realize that creativity was the core of everything this author did: creative financing, creative ways of managing a house, and creative choices.

I know this author very well. She is my Mom.

Christmas was truly a sign of her creativity. She shopped every month for Christmas, put the gifts in a locked closet and by November, she was finished. She never gave us allowances, but rather waited until two weeks before Christmas and had a gift exchange for us. We had to make something from found objects for the person whose name we pulled. Then, she would give us an envelope filled with money to buy gifts for friends and family.

Her entertainment was creative also. In the summer, after coming home from work, she would sometimes put our supper and toys into a picnic basket, then take us to the park to run and play. Sometimes we would go to the movies at the library. All these activities were free.

In spite of her creativity, however, until now, I did not know my mother had to overcome many fears: that no one would care for her children if something happened to her; she had several babysitters lined up just in case one did not show, which was almost every week; and if her job shut down, she would be unable to give us a decent life. Several people also tried to keep her from purchasing her first home because they thought she could not handle a new home and four children. She owned the house for 30 years and never missed a payment. She ran her house on her strengths and not her weaknesses.

Mom also came up with ways to keep us busy while she was at work. We had to volunteer at various places, such as hospitals, the library, etc.

This book will show what fear is and how to overcome it. The author thanks her Mother, but I, too, must thank the person whom I now know so well—the author of this book, my Mom, for teaching us not to be afraid to create. Thanks, Mom.

Tammi Jo Haynes

PREFACE

Ever since I was a toddler, I always had the freedom to play, explore, and make decisions. I had never been exposed to people who interfered or told me what I should and should not do. After I became an adult, however, it was a different world. People began to tell me that at a certain age, I should not do this or that because of my "age" or because other people did not do it.

I realized then that they put restrictions on others because of their own beliefs, attitudes, and backgrounds. There is only one reason why they feel uncomfortable when you do something different—their own fears. Whether it is business or the arts, people do not create because they are afraid to do so.

ACKNOWLEDGMENT

Before I go any further, I must dedicate this section to my mother who did something very extraordinary when I was a child. She let me make my own decisions, suffer the consequences, and never interfered with my mental or physical space. As far as my mental space, for instance, she never restricted me and never said, "Don't do this or don't do that". Regarding my physical space, I sometimes sat in the doorway while I painted pictures and she would just walk around me. I did not know what she was doing until one day I heard her say, "Always give children their space." It wasn't until I was grown that I understood she allowed me to be inquisitive, then test and explore my environment. In the end, I would usually figure out problems I had with my projects. This was indeed a recipe for a creative child.

I now compare my mother to someone who was babysitting me when I was about five years old. As usual, just like I did at home, I picked up some items and began experimenting and enjoying my space. That is, until the "babysitter" entered the room and said, "Can't you see the mess you're making? Look around you."

I looked around me and for the first time, saw cut paper all over the floor. I was so focused on my project I did not see the mess that is associated with creating.

When my mother came to take me home, I said, "Momma, she said I was making a mess."

My mother in all her wisdom said, "Barbara, everybody doesn't let you play like I do." Looking back at that incident, I realize that some people did not understand the creative process as my mother did. Until that time, I had never been exposed to all the negative comments that are linked with creativity.

By then, however, it was too late. I already had the strength to overcome negative attitudes. That babysitter's comment actually made me stronger. I had no problem experimenting with new ideas and different objects. I realize now that it was the babysitter's fears—not mine.

That incident also showed me that some people are usually derailed and distracted by the things going around them while others focused on the project at hand. For your wisdom, your insight, ***Thank You, Mom***.

INTRODUCTION

With modern technology, it seems almost unbelievable that creativity should be an issue. However, even now, in spite of the fact people are exposed to terms such as: e-mails, blogs, iPods, twitter, tweets, and dozens, maybe hundreds of 21st century technical terms, most people that I have met are still afraid of creativity. They still call you negative names if you even think differently from them. Yet, these very people carry around the latest computer-generated equipment. They don't seem to realize that someone had to take that first step of being called "weird, stupid, or crazy" in order to invent the very things in use today.

Inventors had to step over the negative comments in order to do something different. These are the brave, those who are willing to jump into that unsafe area of something new. This is a "how to" book to prepare those who want to create, but are apprehensive.

Hopefully, after reading this book, you will be strong enough to overcome the reality that people will put obstacles in your way when you do anything against the "norm" whether it is the arts or business.

After conducting art workshops, I realized there was a need to write this book. I observed that the participants were painting or drawing things that were "safe" and took no risks. It was difficult for them to break loose from "tradition".

The cover of my book shows the things that keep people from creating and the fact that they want to stay in the acceptable and safe area and they want to be like everyone else. There is only one thing that keeps anyone from creating—fear.

In some cities the residents are care-free and have thrown off the restraints of society. They have an "anything-goes" attitude, and seem to have no restraints as to what they will do. Then, there are those in other cities that are traditional, conservative and don't want to "rock the boat". They will do what the average person does so they will not stand out in a crowd.

As a word of caution, though, everything that is different is not necessarily creative. Therefore, I felt compelled to add a section, "The Thin Line", which encourages you to test the boundaries to see if you have gone too far. In other words, there is a period of time when you need to take a project in a different direction because there is a thin line between creativity and destruction.

THE FULL NEST

"I found it!!!" I wanted to shout and let the world know. I jumped—no leaped—out of the car. At last!! There it was. A wooden crate lying on the pile of dirt weathered by the rain and snow.

That day was THE day to make something from a wooden crate, which will be shown later. I wanted to do this since I was about six years old, but did not have the know-how and when I got older, and had four children, I did not have the time. My younger son had graduated from school and was on his own. I knew I had to do it. My life would certainly be no empty nest. It would be filled with things I wanted to create all my life. Little did I realize, however, that the road to filling that nest would now be overcrowded with all types of barriers.

As I dragged the crate into the house, others heard about what I was doing. I could already hear the verbal abuse:

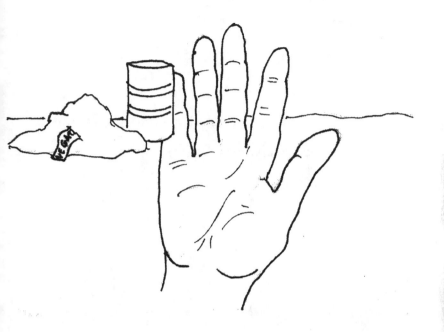

"What is she doing now?" someone asked in disgust.

"Gotta be something weird," someone else said.

"Yeah, she's always doing something different."

I closed the door to shut out the downbeat comments.

"What's going on over there?"

"Something strange."

I felt as though I drove onto a rocky road filled with large rocks and traps of open manholes filled with overburdening negativity.

If you are an artist of any media, you have probably heard some or all of these comments. Or maybe you yourself are guilty of saying this to artists, dancers, musicians who perform something you have never seen or heard before.

And then, there's the other side of the fence. The people who think you are creative, but they tolerate you because, in their minds, you were born weird, strange, or different. But, wait a minute. Aren't those the same things that were said about famous artists, inventors, and other innovators of the past?

Those creators apparently rose above the average way of thinking. They had a destination and would let little or nothing stop them.

To overcome an enemy, however, first it must be identified and its weak points exposed. The enemy in this case is Fear. The weak point is that it has no control or power over you. I learned sometime ago that it is not what people do to you, but how you handle it. In this case, there is nothing you can do to stop people from calling you names. You can, however, decide how you want to react to their comments. You also have the power not to allow anyone to affect your goals, and believe me, there will be many roadblocks on the way to success and creativity.

<u>How does Fear look?</u> To paraphrase several dictionaries, it is "anticipated". In other words, it has not happened yet. It could be in the form of . . . well, it's best if I let you hear it.

"Bite! Bite!", screamed the toddler I was babysitting. I turned around. His eyes were like big, wide circles.

I looked down on the floor where he was pointing.

"Bite! Bite!" he screamed again.

"No, baby. It's not going to bite," I assured him as I picked up the green fuzzy stuffed animal that fell from the closet. I gently took his hand and we both rubbed the stuffed animal together.

"Bite," he whispered. Then he carried it around with him several times that day.

Fear is not real because it's something we think will happen. It is all perceived. Anticipated. We seem to equate it to things that frighten us the most. Like a mouse. Okay. I have fears, too. But, I was not as verbal as the toddler.

One day, I tried to maintain my composure as I stared at the wastebasket.

"Kenny!!" I called my son. "There's a mouse near the wastebasket. It's not moving, so it might be dead."

He ran over to the wastebasket, looking quite stunned with his mouth open. He'll take care of it, I thought.

He bent over and . . . oh, no! He picked it up.

Now I'm verbal.

I ran as he threw it into the air. I yelled—no, screamed.

"Mama's scared of a scouring pad. Mama's scared of a scouring pad," he sang. I knew I should have had my glasses on.

You see, it was not a mouse at all that scared me, but rather the anticipation—the perception that I thought it was a mouse. In reality, though, it was nothing but a scouring pad.

It is the same as people who are afraid when you create something they don't understand so they proceed to develop their own story—their own thoughts about what you are doing then they put obstacles in your way to stop you.

Several parents, because of their own insecurities, taught their children not to be creative. When children worked on projects that the parents did not understand, they would tell them to "Stop doing that. You have to do what other people do. If you don't, people will call you weird".

In effect, they were teaching the children to be traditional, rigid, don't take calculated risks, and to follow the crowd and be average.

If you, too, hesitate to do something different, the following information should help remove obstacles and give you the strength to overcome people's negative remarks. Remember, it should be their fears—not yours.

Make no mistake, though. There is a difference between people who put stumbling blocks in your way and those who make suggestions and are knowledgeable about your project. There is also a difference between people "supporting" you and "agreeing" with you. I may support your idea of building a house, but I will not agree with your idea of building the house out of newspaper. You don't have to take that advice, but good common sense and guidance can save you time, money, and resources.

OBSTACLES

There are anxieties on both sides. Those who create are afraid that the following obstacles will be used against them. Those who do not create will use those same barriers to stop someone from doing something different:

- ◆ Laughter: a weapon that others use to keep you from going forward with your creation.

- ◆ Tradition: something that the average person will fight to keep.

- ◆ Safety in Numbers: People feel safe when they ban together against the person who is different from them. In this case, anyone who shows any sign of creativity.

- ◆ Sticks and Stones (also known as "name-calling"): weird, crazy, and strange are names designed to hurt and keep you "average" or "normal".

♦ Misunderstanding: Society as a whole sometimes does not take art seriously and think it's done just because you have nothing else to do.

♦ Closed minds are rigid: If it hasn't been done before, don't do it.

♦ Isolation: Many times when creating, you may have to stand alone.

HOW TO REMOVE FEAR:

The following three steps will help you pry yourself loose from the things that block you from creating: the tools, the test, and the key.

STEP 1. Tools:

To remove or build anything, you must first have the proper tools. In this case, the who, what, when, where, and why of creativity;

(a) Who is creative? That can be answered in one word: Everyone. It is my strong belief that we are all born to create any and everything from business to sports to the arts. That is our gift so we can survive and grow. There are many examples that even those who are or have been incarcerated are highly creative. A prisoner, for instance, once made a gun from soap. Another inmate used dental floss to saw away the prison bars to escape. A criminal can find more ways to get into your house than you can. They have all the signs of creativity: the patience to watch your habits, the risk they take to break into your house, and the determination to strip you of your belongings. They just use their creativity in the wrong way.

(b) What do you create? Music, visual arts, a business? Performing and visual arts are obviously creative. However, a business can also be creative, but do you know when you've gone too far? (See "The Thin Line," p. 37).

(c) When does a person begin to create? From the time you can walk, the process begins. With few exceptions, children seem naturally curious and begin pulling things out of a cupboard or banging things on surfaces because they are just learning and exploring the world around them. Adults on the other hand somewhere along life's road, want to fit into society and, therefore, seem to have more fears than children. Children seem to take more risks, even though at times, of course, they need some guidelines for their own safety. If you see a child for instance, exploring an electrical outlet, there is some need for limitations and guidelines. (See "The Thin Line." p. 37)

(d) Where? Everywhere. We should create in the house, at school, at the store, your yard, in the car, or the bus, while playing, working, etc. The whole world should be your inspiration. But again, discipline and common sense should prevail. Know when you should experiment. For instance, if you're driving, it is not safe to drive while writing, painting, etc.

(e) Why do we create? That is our way to move forward, and survive. Without creation, we would still be stuck in cavemen days.

Progress came, however, when some cavemen realized that they could make stones into tools. Tools became machines. Machines became electronics. Cars were invented because there was a need to move faster.

The airplane was invented because there was a need and curiosity to connect with the world.

We also make things out of necessity, but we must first remove the fear that gets in the way. For example, one day I could not find my ponytail combs. So, I took a couple of shower curtain hooks and put them in my hair. The hooks worked just fine, until one of them slipped and my co-worker said in disbelief, "I can't believe what you're wearing in your hair."

"Whatever works," I said. At that point, the name-calling started.

"That's weird. That's crazy", she said.

"You have a lot of fears, don't you?" I asked her. "I can tell you've never made decisions for yourself. You've been controlled all of your life, and that made you afraid to do things on your own." She hesitated then told me how her father, brothers and uncle always told her what to do. Then, after she got married, her husband and sons controlled her. She thought for a moment and then admitted that what I said was true.

Then a few days later, she ran into my office all excited. As if she got a taste of freedom, she truly earned the title of "weird, crazy, and strange". "You'll be so proud of me. Look what I found to put in my hair."

She proudly showed me something that looked like nuts and bolts in her hair.

I gave her the okay sign and smiled with approval. "Keep it up. You're going to be just like me."

STEP 2. The Test:

Most people I know are not brave enough to do anything different from what is acceptable to society. When you go down that untraveled path, you and your project will be called crazy, stupid, looney and, well, you know the routine.

There are four parts to the test to see if you are afraid to create. Give yourself 20 seconds for each question. No peeking.

a. The Challenge. If I were to give you some lace or denim, what is the most creative thing you would do with that material?

Okay. Time is up.

b. The key to the door of creativity. Now, put that lace or denim somewhere it has never been before. Will you throw away the key and not even think about what's behind that door? Or will you jump in feet or head first and take that risk? Or will you go too far?

c. What I would do. Now is the time to tell you what I will do with that lace or denim because I threw off those traditional ideas. I will put it somewhere it has never been before. Hold onto your seats. I'm going to do something scary, something unique.

I have to be ready to endure the harassment, the name-calling and even bullying trying to bring me back to "tradition and average".

Here we go.

I would put the lace on a BRICK!!

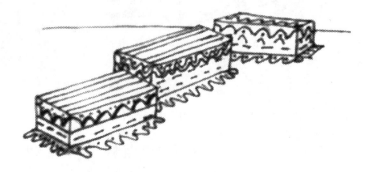

[GASP!!] Oh, no. Here comes the laughter, the ridicule, and/or one of these remarks: "What made her do something like that? Why, that's never been done before. That's strange! Stupid! She always does something that nobody else does. She's so different. You know it had to be something weird." Or just as bad: "She's so creative or talented". My answer to the latter is that I am no more talented than anyone else. I just don't have the fears that the average person has.

Why in the world would I put lace on a brick? Well, I could make a social issue out of it. It could represent the delicate nature of a person up against the hard knocks of society. Or, I could spray paint the lace the same color of the brick, make a sculpture and put it in my gallery.

At this point, I must be ready to stand alone. I have jumped into that area of uncertainty, that place where people will begin the name-calling. Keep focused, though.

STEP 3. The Unlocked Door

Now that I have given you the key, will you be able to use it? Are you brave and strong enough to endure the bad attitudes and drive on that unstable road of tradition, bullying, harassment, laughter and condemnation to use that key to open the door of creativity?

Let's return to the Challenge above. Now, are you able to take that lace or denim and put it somewhere it has never been before?

Just as an experiment, after a contractor laid down my new sidewalk, I couldn't resist it. I gave him the key to create. He hesitated for a minute. I could see he was still struggling, trying to break free. Then as if to gain a burst of strength, he said, "I know what I would do. I'll mix some cement, drag the lace through it, then wrap the lace around the cement and have it coming off the edge."

"YES!! You made it," I clapped and jumped up and down. He yelled, "I feel so free!!"

Will you join him? Will you take that same ride as your fellow risk-takers?

THE COMPANY YOU SHOULD KEEP

Whenever you do something new or different, you may feel alone. However, since time began, all creatures, civilized or otherwise, human or inhuman are creative. This is our survival technique and where we learn to constantly improve and move forward. It is competitive. It is rough. It is a scary, sometimes lonesome fight to do something new, innovative, different and better. You will be in that risky area, the unknown.

Those risks, however, must be calculated and well thought-out. Have a safety net, a backup plan before jumping into that muddy, murky ditch. Learn from those who failed and hold hands with those who made it.

Are you willing to join inventors of the past? Just remember, when you are in despair, get on board. You are in good company.

You, in fact, will be among those inventors, philosophers, artists, who took that first step.

Galileo was going to be executed for saying that the earth rotated around the Sun. Later, society found his theory was true.

The Wright brothers were called "looney" and people laughed at the very thing that helps connect us to the world—the airplane.

Sarah E. Goode was faced with daunting effects of being a slave; yet was brave enough to apply for and receive a patent for a cabinet bed (roll-away-bed).

Thomas Edison's mother was going to send him to a psychiatrist because even though he was experimenting, he kept blowing up buildings.

Henry Ford had to endure comments such as, "I don't know why he is building that stupid contraption". You know, the thing that gets us to the store and work—the car.

As you can see, when you do anything that people have never seen or heard before, you are among the most ingenious past and current artists, inventors and other trendsetters. They had the strength and determination to overcome those who could not see the future. You are indeed in good company: the masters and mistresses of courage and determination.

Motor Car? Ain't gonna do nothin' but scare the horses!!

THE THIN LINE

How can you tell if your business or art is creative or destructive?

Would you open a business that made shoes just for the right foot? That's different, but is it creative? Is it profitable? Owning a store that only sells green fingernail polish is different, but is it cost-effective? Would people buy green fingernail polish regularly? According to Ellen Glasgow, "All change is not growth [just] as all movement is not forward".

The point is that if you're not careful, you will overstep that boundary—that thin line—between creativity and destruction.

For instance, a restaurant owner in Toledo routinely stopped some unsuspecting customers at the door after they ate and they were ready to leave. He would accuse them of stealing silverware from the restaurant. He frisked them and sure enough, they had silverware in their pockets. After embarrassing them and showing the other customers that he caught the "thieves", everyone had a good laugh because the regular customers knew that the owner planted silverware in a customer's coat pocket while the coat was hanging on the hangers. People went to the restaurant not only for good food, but also to see the practical joke played on the innocent unwary customer.

Yesteryear, that was a creative business and might be all right during that period of time. Today, however, the customer might sue for defamation of character or other damages and the joke might be on the owner. It is a good idea, then, to consider the period of time. What was acceptable in the 20th century may not be tolerable in the 21st century.

My point is that there is a thin line between creativity and destruction. Creative means to build. Destruction means to tear down. When you cross that threshold and move from creativity to destruction, you have gone too far. For instance, if I put lace on that brick that I described above and used it for my art gallery to make a social statement, that would be creative.

However, if I took hundreds of those lace bricks and built a house with them that would be destructive for several reasons:

1. Neighbors might complain because it could devalue their properties.

2. If I lived in a historic district, the City could charge me heavy fines and possibly sue me.

3. My house could possibly be harder to sell. Or in the alternative, I would probably have to allow an extra discount as a redecorating fee so the buyer can remove the lace bricks. In other words, know when to stop. Criticize yourself and be honest. Ask yourself, "Is this going to take me backwards?"

I know. I know. When it comes to the art world, you probably think there should be no boundaries; otherwise, it's censorship. I agree. Art is usually subjective. What is gross, objectionable or offensive to one person is not to another person. However, the very fact it is subjective, as an artist, you should be able to critique your own work.

As an artist myself, I have to feel comfortable with the paintings I exhibit. I have to know what audience I want to reach (the elderly, young, female, male, etc.). Do I want to draw them to me so I can get my point across? I do take many risks, but I don't want to scare my audience away because these are the very people I want to embrace my idea—my concept.

How comfortable artists feel about their work and subject matter, in my opinion, makes them the ultimate judge what to exhibit. In the end, though, the public will decide whether you win or lose, whether they want to purchase your artwork or use your service.

Speaking of the art world and business, my favorite artist of all times is Caravaggio whose work, in my opinion, looked similar to that of Rembrandt's. However, it was not so much his artwork that attracted me to him. Rather, it was the fact that in those days, anything that dealt with religion had to be beautiful, contain plenty of gold and show little or no emotions. He rebelled and painted his street friends—real people with emotions in religious scenes and painted the Virgin Mary without shoes, which was a no-no in those days. He was rejected by the art world and never sold a painting. I like his risk-taking, his radical nature. It was that same defiance, however, that kept getting him into trouble.

More information can be found about Caravaggio from his prison records than from his artwork. In other words, he not only rebelled in the art world, but also in his day-to-day life. So, even though creativity should be fearless, there are times when you should exhibit self-discipline and conform to rules and regulations.

I am sure you see where I'm headed with this. Every person goes through this highway—this uphill path of negativity when they enter the Creative Zone—that place where some people will not go without a fight.

Are you able to release the locks that keep you from creating and struggle on that bumpy pathway full of Caution and Stop signs? Or will you search for that safe area where there are no challenges, no calculated risks?

Come on. You have the map, the tools, and the key to unlock the door to creativity.

And you are not alone.

There is plenty of Good Company. It's a rough ride.

Your obstacle: Fear. Your destination: Creativity.

AFTER THE LAUGHTER:
WHAT I MADE FROM THE CRATE

Despite the laughter, negative comments, and name-calling, I made the found object—the crate—into my long-awaited precious dollhouse. Most of the furniture was bought. However, I filled the balance of the house with treasured found objects made into handmade miniatures: material from my children's clothes became a quilt; a piece of handmade soap from my first granddaughter when she was about nine years old became a piece of soap in the dollhouse bathroom; my other granddaughter who at the time, was eight years old, wrote a note to put on the refrigerator; and sheets and pillow cases were made from the last sheet my sons slept on before they left home on their own. In other words, these objects which otherwise would have been tossed away and homeless, I built them a place called a home, in the form of the Doll House.

From twisted wire made into clothes hangers to discarded wrist watches made into clocks, this was my risky venture—my long-awaited crate. Full of memories—my life. An excerpt from the poem, "The Reconstruction" I wrote about this long-awaited crate says it all:

> "Indeed I'm made of scraps of wood;
>   and I look that way, you see;
> but don't look on the outside
>   Just what's inside of me.
> So, in spite of odds against her
>   With toiling and with strife,
> With sheer determination
>   The artist brought me back to life."

<u>THE END.</u>

<u>OR IS IT THE BEGINNING?</u>

Close-up of Dollhouse Kitchen.

AUTHOR'S NOTES

I was always fascinated with finding objects and making projects out of them. I felt the objects were useful at one time, but once they were broken, old or no longer served a purpose, they were tossed aside. I felt those discarded still had a purpose. So, I would incorporate these objects into my artwork. At first, people thought it was "weird", but I persisted and would not allow anyone to discourage me.

Now while pursuing my Bachelor's Degree in fine arts, I have exhibits throughout the City, in my home gallery, and when I conduct workshops. Now, people are beginning to understand the concept of found objects and even lavish me with more of the same (minus the laughter).

This book can be inspirational and helpful when conducting various seminars—whether they are for business or the arts. Therefore, to be creative, you must be ready for adversity in all of your aspirations. Those traits of strength and determination apply not only to all artistic ventures, but also in business.

The painting on the cover[1] is the one used to begin my workshops. I told my class that I am no more creative than they are. Creating means doing something different and when they do that, only the dread of laughter keeps them from pursuing their goals and dreams.

From my teenage years to adulthood, I taught everything from shorthand and typing to 7-12 year olds to artwork to those who never touched a canvas.

There are two students, though, that I treasure to this day. My father who was in a nursing home is one of them. I asked him to go to the recreation class to

---

[1] *"Create" is 36" x 37" on birchwood with a circle 24" circumference, and 3/16" thick attached to the mid-section of the painting. Real rusted chains are attached.*

participate in an art project. He was afraid to try, but I encouraged and applauded him as he picked up his pencil and said, "I haven't done anything like this since I was in Kindergarten." I still treasure the project he made.

The other student I taught was my mother and convinced her to paint three pictures of her life: the log cabin where she was delivered by a mid-wife; the tent in which she lived; and an abstract picture of a woman washing clothes on a washboard. They both left a part of themselves behind. She was proud of her work just as my father was proud of his. And so am I.

Sharing information is the driving force for me to teach and to write this book. Just as my Mom and Dad left an unusual gift for me, I feel honored to leave my experiences to help others overcome their fears and for them to absorb the knowledge and strength needed to drive down that bumpy, challenging, scary, sometimes lonesome road, called Creativity.